THE FURIOUS NOTEBOOK

By Martha Rich

Release Your Rage, Use Your Anger for Good, and Chill the Heck Out

CHRONICLE BOOKS
SAN FRANCISCO

ISBN: 978-1-4521-7500-3

Manufactured in China.

Design by Alma Kamal.
10 9 8 7 6 5 4 3 2 1

Chronicle books and gifts are available at special quantity discounts to
corporations, professional associations, literacy programs, and other
organizations. For details and discount information, please contact our
premiums department at corporatesales@chroniclebooks.com or at
1-800-759-0190.

Chronicle Books LLC
680 Second Street
San Francisco, California 94107
www.chroniclebooks.com

INTRODUCTION

You wouldn't be reading this if it wasn't for rage. I wouldn't be writing this if it wasn't for fury. The pictures in this book wouldn't exist if it wasn't for anger.

It all started a long time ago in a small one-bedroom Brentwood apartment in Los Angeles. My husband of one year and I had friends from Atlanta visiting for the weekend. After a nice dinner and drinks out, we settled in for the night, our friends ensconced on the pullout couch in the living room. As we were falling asleep, my husband turned to me and said, "I've done you wrong," and proceeded to tell me he was having an affair. Blindsided and reeling and unable to react due to our guests sleeping on the other side of the wall, I pushed the feelings of hurt and rage deep inside and finished out the weekend with a smile on my face.

Let's just say after our friends left the volcano blew and my inner *Jerry Springer Show* guest spewed hot lava over everything. I screamed and yelled and threw his clothes out into the courtyard. I cried and kicked him out and begged him to come back and kicked him out again and drank bottles of wine alone while listening to Hole in the fetal position on the floor.

It was the first time I had really expressed outward anger and emotion since I was a kid throwing temper tantrums. My status quo is holding emotion and anger in. This was so out of control, my body was like, "What the hell, Lady!?" It gave me stomach pains so bad I went to the hospital. They thought I had appendicitis and kept me overnight. Needless to say, going into exploding-volcano mode is not the best way to deal with rage.

Even after the hospital stay, the anger ate me up. It was all-consuming and not pretty. Being pissed off at everything wasn't making things better, nor was the rage subsiding. I wanted a healthier way to express it, so I started drawing in a sketchbook and writing my anger down. The stuff I drew and wrote was super embarrassing. I cringe thinking about it, but it was how I came to the realization that doing all the things you were "supposed" to do—go to college, get a job, get married, be a good wife, blah blah blah—didn't actually lead to happily ever after. I said to myself, "F this shit. I am going to do what I want to do." I started taking night classes in illustration because I always loved to draw, and it seemed like a cool idea. Later with the encouragement of some great teachers, I quit my cubicle job and went back to art school full time to become an illustrator. My life is much better for it.

Without all that rage, I would not have taken that leap. I am too wimpy. Writing down what I was feeling and making no-holds-barred-rage art helped me be stronger. I was the boss of it. It was no longer the boss of me. I faced the fury instead of letting it wreck me.

Since then, and I have gone to marches and protests, met new people, joined action groups, canvassed, phone-banked, and I even ran for office and WON! I credit using the art I made in a fit of anger on my campaign material as the reason I won and got the most votes. Art made me stand out from the other candidates. Anger is now my muse.

Hopefully this book will help you harness your fury to make good changes. Being free to express it in these pages may open you up to new ideas, see what is really making you mad, help you face something, or just calm you down so you don't do something you regret. Ha! Anger can be a heavy load on your back, but it can also push you forward. It is how you deal with it that makes the difference.

I still use my anger to make things happen—the most recent rage-inducer being the 2016 election. I cannot begin to express the fury it caused me. My sketchbooks are filled with expletives and angry rantings and ugly drawings. I am still struggling with it, but taking action helped. Working it out in my sketchbook felt good. You get to control the narrative and be all powerful. It lifted the paralysis that feeling helpless can create.

Now I realize there are different levels of anger and different reasons to be angry. Some are really serious and should be worked through with a professional. This book is more for the everyday anger of life. It's a place to vent, rant, create, and calm down enough to do something about it. The main thing is to not hold it in until it explodes.

HOW TO USE THIS BOOK

A lot of times we get angry at something, push it aside, and tuck it into our anger reserves. Then something new pisses us off and we do it again. Push repeat until the reserves are bursting and they explode like a volcano. Put the fury into this book instead of in your reserves. Use it as your own personal anti-anger-suppression tool. Or maybe you are one of those people who gets pissed and lashes out instantly without thinking. Maybe that gets you into trouble. Open this book before you lash out. Use it as your count-to-ten slow down.

Since anger is not all the same, this book is divided up into different levels of anger: Slightly Perturbed for the low-level irritations; Super Annoyed for when you get too many low-level irritations in a row; Pissed Off for the bigger issues; Seething Anger for when you can't let it go; and Red Hot Fury for when you are going to blow. There's a Chill the Heck Out section, too.

Start this book wherever you want because there is no order to rage. It comes and goes as it pleases. It can start at the Red Hot Fury level and switch to Pissed Off in an instant. Hop in at whatever level you want.

Draw, vent, rant, scream, deface, or just write it all down. After you've cooled off, go back and look at what you wrote or drew. Contemplate. Do the exercises, ask different questions, write some more, do whatever you need to do.

It's a place to wrestle with your anger demons and weaken them, or use them to make something happen.

SLIGHTLY PERTURBED

PET PEEVES

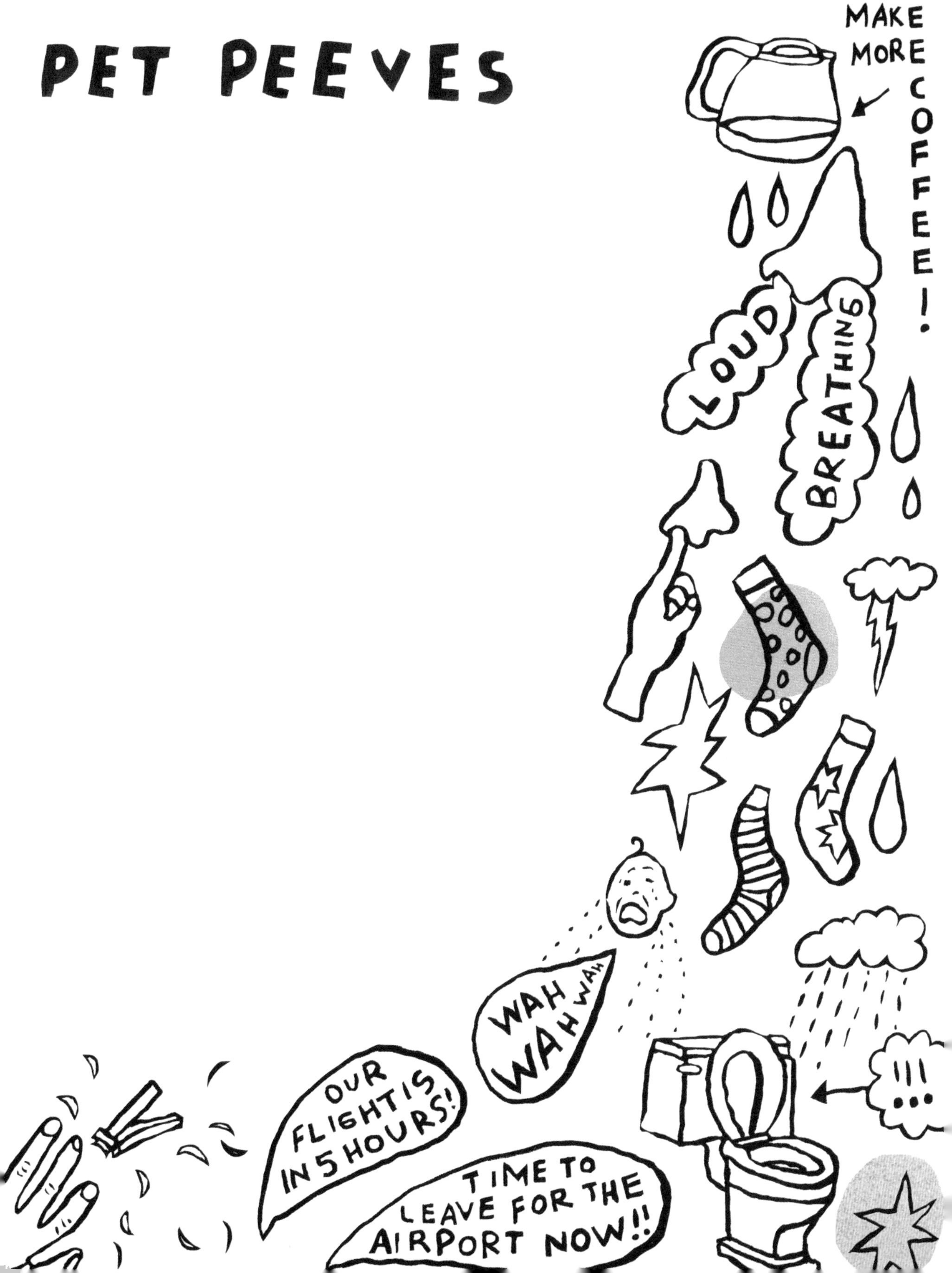
MAKE MORE COFFEE!
LOUD BREATHING
WAH WAH WAH WAH
!!! •••
OUR FLIGHT IS IN 5 HOURS!
TIME TO LEAVE FOR THE AIRPORT NOW!!

WRITE

SOMETHING SWEET

DRAW YOUR PERTURBED FACE

DECORATE YOUR CRANKY PANTS

VENT

"THE TRUTH WILL
SET YOU FREE, BUT
FIRST IT WILL PISS
YOU OFF."
GLORIA
STEINEM

WHAT MAKES YOU LESS PERTURBED?

"WHEN ANGRY COUNT TO TEN BEFORE YOU SPEAK. IF VERY ANGRY COUNT TO ONE HUNDRED."
THOMAS JEFFERSON

NO

DRAW
THINGS
TO SAY
NO TO

YOU CAN'T SHAKE HANDS WITH A CLENCHED FIST.

LIST THINGS

THAT ANNOY YOU

VENT

WRITE

FILL THESE
PAGES WITH
THE NAMES
OF PEOPLE
OR THINGS
THAT NEED TO

TALK
TO THE
HAND

WHAT DO YOU DO THAT IS ANNOYING?

DRAW
YOUR
ANNOYED
FACE

ANGER IS ONE
LETTER SHORT
OF DANGER.

LIST ANNOYING
THINGS PEOPLE SAY

LET
IT GO

LOVE

WRITE

THINGS THAT PISS ME OFF

JUDGY PEOPLE

OUT OF COFFEE

RANT HERE

GO OUTSIDE AND

BREAK A PLATE

OR WRITE INSTEAD

WRITE IT
DOWN
TEAR IT
UP
THROW
IT
AWAY

SNAPPY COMEBACKS
YOU WISH YOU SAID

IT'S OK TO
BE ANGRY

WRITE IT DOWN

WHAT DO YOU
DO THAT
PISSES
PEOPLE OFF?

DRAW WHAT
ANGER LOOKS
LIKE TO YOU.

RANT

RAVE

WHEN
YOU ARE
SEETHING

ASK
ANOTHER
QUESTION

WHO?
WHAT?
WHY?

"THERE ARE SOME THINGS YOU LEARN BEST IN CALM. SOME IN STORM".

WILLA CATHER

WHAT HAS
ANGER DONE
FOR YOU?

MY ENTIRE LIFE IS DEEPLY INFORMED BY RAGE, FEAR, BEAUTY, AND LOVE.

IT MADE ME STAND UP FOR MYSELF

I AVOID ALL HUMANS

YOU AND A FRIEND
GRAB SOME
PAPER.
WRITE DOWN
YOUR ANGER.
TRADE.
WRITE DOWN 5
SOLUTIONS.
TRADE BACK.
DISCUSS.

ANGER IS MY MUSE

DRAW YOUR MUSE

"DON'T
JUST SIT
THERE
STEWING.
DO SOMETHING."

MY MOM

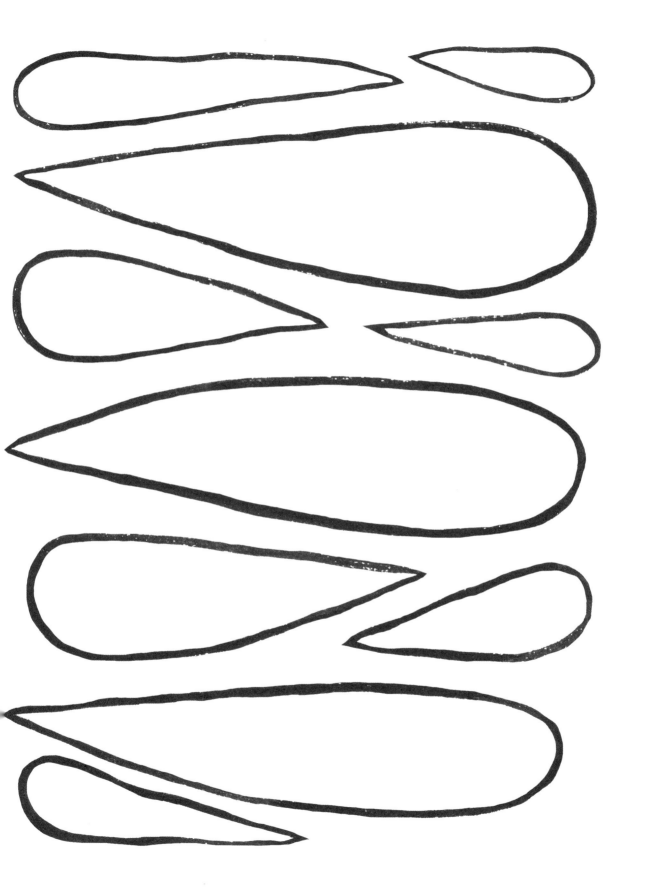

RED HOT FURY

"WHEN ANGRY, COUNT
TO FOUR; WHEN VERY
ANGRY, SWEAR. UNDER
CIRCUMSTANCES,
  URGENT CIRCUMSTANCES,
DESPERATE
  CIRCUMSTANCES,
  PROFANITY PROVIDES
RELIEF DENIED EVEN
  TO PRAYER."
        MARK TWAIN

SWEAR

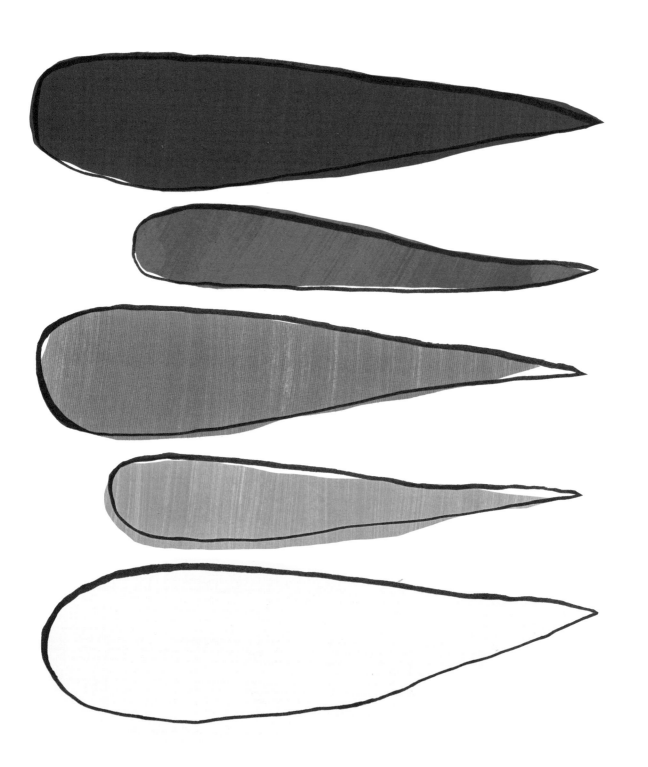

LET HER RIP

INJUSTICE
IS THE #1
THING THAT
MAKES ME
RAGE.

YOU DON'T HAVE TO SHOW THIS TO ANYONE. BE CORNY AS HELL IF YOU WANT.

DRAW YOURSELF AS A SUPERHEROINE OR HERO.

"HOLDING ON TO ANGER IS LIKE GRASPING A HOT COAL WITH THE INTENT OF THROWING IT AT SOMEONE ELSE: YOU ARE THE ONE WHO GETS BURNED."

BUDDHA

WHAT HAS FURY DONE FOR YOU?

WRITE
10 THINGS
YOU CAN CHANGE

DON'T JUST SIT THERE STEW-ING. TAKE ACTION.

LIST ACTION ITEMS FOR MAKING CHANGE HAPPEN

PROVE THEM
WRONG

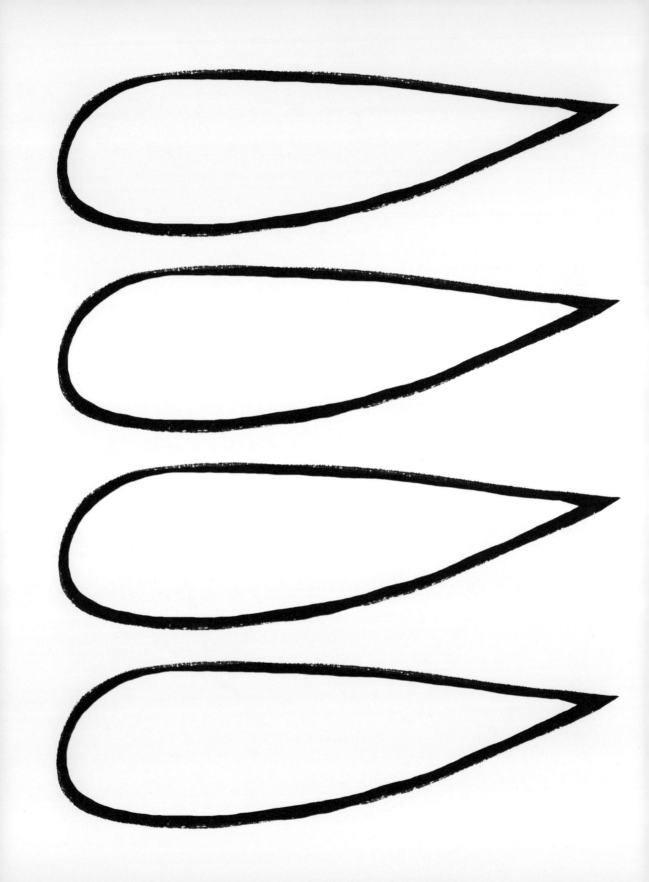

DRAW YOUR RAGE FACE

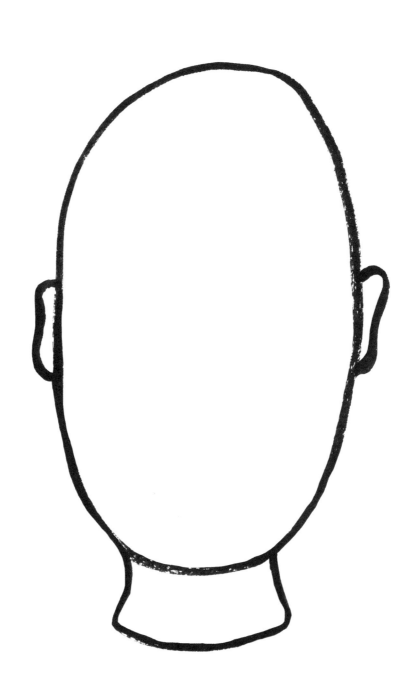

CHILL THE HECK OUT

WHAT MAKES YOU CHILL OUT?

BUNNIES

SEX

MAKING ART

HUGS

THE BEACH

A BATH

COLD COFFEE

FOOD

HUGS FROM PEOPLE I LOVE

COOPERATION AND FRIEND-SHIP

15 MINUTES OF WALLOWING

RUN

NATURE

REAL HOUSE WIVES

SOUP

DA CL

REA

A DAY OFF NO RUSH

BOOZE

A GOOD NIGHT'S SLEEP

CATS WINE COOL PEOPLE

MY DOG

OGA

ALONE TIME

A MOUNTAIN STREAM

ALONE WITH A TV AND SOME CHOCOLATE

WORKING IN THE STUDIO

TE

MEDITATING

MONEY

LATE NIGHT TALKS WITH FRIENDS

STARING AT THE WAVES

WHAT ARE YOU
GOING TO
WORK ON?

MAKE A COMIC ABOUT

CALMING THE HELL DOWN

ACT

"LET US GO FORTH WITH
FEAR AND COURAGE
AND RAGE TO SAVE
THE WORLD."
GRACE PALEY

WRITE YOUR GOALS

IT'S
OK TO
ASK
FOR
HELP
IF YOU
NEED IT

ANGER IS MY DRIVING FORCE.

LOVE

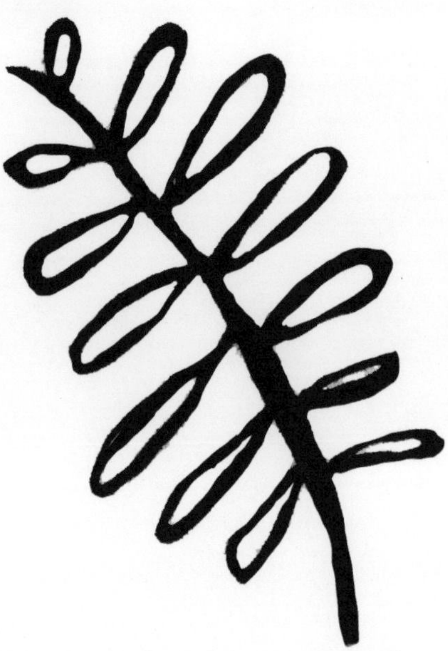